ONLINE BUSINESS MODELS

A Bird-eye View of Online Business

Dario Gallione

SUMMARY

Introduction

As most know, there is a myriad of different methods of producing personal income online. Online business models are all very similar to those that you are familiar with in the offline world. Online merchants can sell goods and services, sell information, produce or promote products for wholesale distribution, advertise, consult and much more - just as they can in the offline world. All online business models revolve around the business owner being able to provide products or services that add value to peoples' lives, whether provided on or offline.

In order to start an online business, we should first be able to define exactly what an online business is. There are many variations to what would qualify as an online business. Meaning, that there are many, many, many models that would qualify as being a business.

For our purposes, we're going to use the definition of an online business as: "Any activity conducted online by a person with the intent or purpose to generate a transaction that involves the exchange of information or monetary value."

That's the "stuffy" version of the definition. At least my definition. Proper legal business structure aside, that is the definition we are going to use for the context of this article.

Some of the online business models practically anyone could get started with are: affiliate marketing, Cost Per Action(CPA) marketing (another form of affiliate marketing), lead generation/prospect list building, direct marketing, Multi-Level Marketing (MLM), eCommerce, drop shipping, "domaining," blogging, consulting, providing services to other Internet entrepreneurs, day trading, forex trading and information marketing. To name but a few Internet business models would-be entrepreneurs could choose to pursue.

One of the online business models listed above, is one that many Internet entrepreneurs would argue "isn't a real business." It's the affiliate marketing model. The argument is that since you're not selling your own products or services, you don't have a "real business."

To put that argument to bed, refer back to our definition of an online business model above. Affiliate Marketing, is a real business model because it "generates a transaction that involves the exchange of monetary value" for the originator of the transaction.

As there are a multitude of options for Internet business models, there are also a multitude of ways to get started. Some will require that you have a domain name registered and hosted and a website online with various mechanisms in place to facilitate the generation of transactions, as previously defined.

Other online models don't require a website as the business model could be in generating website traffic that would eventually result in a sale or exchange of information for various product owners and service providers. There are a number of different methods of making money online today. Each different method is a different business model, and your success at making money from home online comes from using a successful model. Think of your online business as a funnel. At the wide side of the funnel you use different methods to attract potential customers to your website or blog. Once they get to your site you provide them some information and try to create sufficient value and trust so that those potential customers will become buyers of your product or service.

The Pay-Per-Click (PPC) or Pay-Per-Action (PPA) models are simple and easy to implement. With these online models, you create advertisements with online sites like Google AdWords. You bid or sometimes pay a fixed price for each click on your ads. When someone clicks one of your ads they're taken to your website or blog where you deliver to them your sales presentation. The advantage of either of these models is that they use a very simple and straight-forward path from attracting the potential customer to making a sale. They can work great for simple market niches in which you're working with commodity products.

For example, a site that sells books can be successful by just getting customers to the site. Some of the potential customers who get there will buy as long as the site makes it easy to buy. The disadvantage is that that PPC or PPA advertising can be difficult to cost justify, and you need to determine the value of a customer and the cost to get each customer to be able to decide if the PPC or PPA models will work for your online business. The objective is to make money from home online obviously, so you need to control your expenses to insure you're getting the desired results.

Another proved online business model is the email marketing model. With this approach you attract potential customers to your site and then get them to sign up for an newsletter or free ebook by entering their email address and possibly some other information like their name. With this information you can deliver additional information with a series of emails to each of these potential customers, eventually delivering a sales presentation.

This is a great model, especially if you're working in a market niche that involves complex subjects. You can demonstrate a thorough knowledge of the subject and an ability to help potential customers solve a problem by delivering quality information. A series of emails using an autoresponder campaign can easily be used to show that knowledge and build trust with your customers. Once that trust is established your customers will be more willing to purchase from you.

The challenge with the email marketing model is that you need to get customers to sign up by giving you their email address. This isn't difficult to do, but it does take some work. And you need to set up and manage an autoresponder account. Fortunately, there is a number of good ones available and the basic concepts of setting up an email marketing campaign are easy to understand.

The Search Engine Optimization (SEO) model is another popular online business model. With this model you work to get your website or blog to the top few positions in the search engine result pages (SERPs) by using on-page and off-page techniques that can improve your site's rankings in the search engines. Those techniques include the use of keywords or search phrases on your site and in the meta data for your site and backlinks from other sites to your site.

When a potential customer searches online for information related to your keyword, they'll see a link to your site on the SERP. The higher your site appears in the SERP listing, the better the chances of the link being clicked by a potential customer. The advantage of the SEO model is that you can improve your site's rank with effort over time to get your site recognized as an expert source of information within your market niche. Once you get to the top of the rankings for a particular search term you'll be rewarded with a steady stream of customers to your site.

The challenge with SEO is that for many it seems to be a black art. Article marketing, backlinking, content creation, and changes by Google in their algorithms mean that you have a solid understanding of what works and what doesn't for your SEO efforts to be effective. You can always pay for help with SEO for your site, but that can be expensive and it's not without risks. There are hundreds of sites on the internet that say they're experts at SEO and can improve your site's ranking instantly. Be extremely careful of such promises. Many (perhaps most) of them are expert only at separating you from your money, and can't possibly deliver on their promises. There are a few legitimate SEO companies and tools that can truly help you. Be sure to investigate thoroughly before If you're making the investment with a correct understanding that it takes times and constant effort to get ranked on the SERPs, then you're likely to be successful with the appropriate action and commitment.

There are other business models in use for online home based businesses. These are just three of the more common ones. And you can always combine these or other models to create a customized model for your business.

The keys to any business model are to keep it simple and to be consistent. Keeping it simple is essential. You should be able to draw your business model on a piece of paper. The drawing should show, from start to finish, how to attract potential customers, take them through the sales process, and turn them into paying customers.

This book is dedicated to giving you the best online business model you can ever imaging from scratch to finish. Enjoy your reading!!!

Simplicity on the other side of complexity

Online business is pretty simple after all - From a Bird's Eye View, at least you can break down the process of online marketing into two main parts:

- What you give
- What you sell

You can do the same for your audience or customer base:

- Your current audience
- Your potential audience

The idea is to both give and sell a lot to both your current and your potential audience. It's easier to sell to your current audience, but important to expand it if you want to make a bigger impact.

Expanding your audience

The way you expand your audience is generally to give. That can come in the form of:

- Videos
- Podcasts
- Articles
- Blogging
- Interviews
- Software (open-source code, limited versions of closed-source software)
- Reports

But giving doesn't just involve letting it sit out there on the World Wide Web. It means actively promoting it and building relationships with people who will want to spread it far and wide. It means pursuing various types of campaigns (e.g. a virtual summit); developing your presence on the major social networks; and generally building your presence online, through developing promotional partnerships, optimizing your site for search engines, and other simple tasks.

The avenues for expanding your audience

Again, the fastest avenue is to develop a campaign, in which you either:

- Spend lots of money and/or

- Get lots of partners on board to promote your campaign.

Other important avenues include developing your presence on social networks, blogging, creating social media, optimizing your site for the search engines, going to conferences and meeting people, and getting generally involved in your community.

The product launch is a very powerful way to give a jumpstart to your business. Here are some product launch ideas (credit to names and ideas goes entirely to Jeff Walker, creator of Product Launch Formula):

- **Quick launch** - If you already have a list, you can simply create a product quickly and then let your list know about it.

- **Seed launch** - If you don't have much of a list, or have a very small one, you ask them what they want and then create it. For example, you could offer several teleseminars to your list, and then sell them later as a product.

- **Internal launch** - This is also for people who have a list, but it's a more drawn out process. You want to build up interest and suspense over time, through previews of content (screenshots, videos, reports, excerpts) and an overall sequence of emails that will generate desire for the product.

- **Big JV (Joint Venture) Launch** - This is where you get as many JVs (partners) as possible to promote your product. It's a complicated and often messy affair, which is why Jeff recommends that you do an internal launch first before going big.

And the last type of launch, which Rich Schefren articulated, is the rolling launch: rather than doing one big (or small) launch, you work with partners and do "micro-launches" to their lists: give away free content, maybe do a teleseminar, and sell the product at the end.

Selling to your audience

The way to sell to your audience is, well, to offer products they want to buy. (The key word here is want: if you're selling things that people don't want to buy, then it's either a bad market or your copywriting isn't working. One way to know if it's a bad market is to, as marketer Frank Kern advises, see if other people are marketing things successfully; if they're not, then it may not be a good market to be in. Of course, if this is your life's work and you know it's what you need to do-and you know that there's a market for what you're doing-then it may be that your marketing isn't doing the trick.)

One way to find out what they want to buy is to ask them. It seems obvious, but it's incredibly important. Ask them what their biggest challenges, questions, and concerns are, what would make their lives easier, what they want to learn most. Use a service like Survey Monkey or Ask Database to do so.

You can sell products like:

- Information (DVDs, CDs, seminars, workshops, retreats, digital audios, videos, and books)

- Subscription access (to software, tutorials, specialized knowledge)

- Anything that people want to buy: art, website templates, you name it

How you make more money with those products is to:

- Develop deeply valuable and trusted relationships with your subscribers. That means giving a lot.

- Offer them more products they want to buy. That means selling as you're giving

- See your business as a Story of Engagement, and think about what it means for the customer to engage with you over time. Where do they start, and where do they end? Once they've ended, are there higher levels at which you can engage with them and products you can offer at those levels.

What do the chapters of that story look like? They tend to follow a similar structure.

Developing lifetime relationships

A lifetime relationship means that someone is so enthralled with you that they have no reason to switch providers. Vance Caesar, who wrote a book entitled The High Achiever's Guide to Happiness, says that healthy relationship are those where each person feels that they are getting more than they are receiving. And that's how your customers need to feel: that the time and financial cost of doing business with you is far less than the benefits they receive from the relationship.

Functionally, in a marketing context, that means three things:

- You're always giving. New reports, blog posts, videos-anything that is useful, interesting, relevant, and remarkable.

- You recommends new products. But when you do recommend new products, either your own or other people's, they must be incredibly relevant to your customers' lives. That is, your customers should thank you for recommending the products that you do.

- Your customers must love you, but what that really means is that you must care about your customers so deeply that they feel you pour your heart and soul into everything you do. Otherwise, you're just another person selling things online.

It also means continuing to roll out new and interesting initiatives that engage your customers-and, of course, that are useful, interesting, relevant, and remarkable. The more you can continue to demonstrate your care, competence, and passion for what you're doing, the more you can develop authentic relationships with your customers.

Now, how do you actually go about making money online?

Increasing (or Initiating) your online revenues

There are several different mechanisms of making money online. Seeing them in an integrated fashion can go a long way toward actually building a business, rather than just a series of disjointed campaigns. One that we don't mention here is advertising; while sponsorships and ads can be a profitable route for some, they are foreign to our own experience, so we have omitted them.

The One-Time Offer (OTO) is when you offer something of value for free: a report, a virtual summit, a series of videos. Then, either on the next page or soon after in the sign-up process (it could be after they confirm their email address with you), you give them a special offer to purchase your product. Often, you'll add a few bonuses for the offer, such as a limited-release report. Be careful, though: this can be obnoxious if done poorly, so make sure to do it with class and integrity.

The continuity program is one of the most powerful models around. Often, this comes through the form of a membership site.

Use autoresponders to help automate your business. An autoresponder is an email marketing technology that enables you to send out emails automatically, regardless of the specific date that the subscriber signs up. For example, if John signs up on April 3rd, and Sally on June 5th, they'll both get your autoresponder messages in the same exact sequence. Some marketers prefer to send 4 or 5 emails over the same number of days, and then continue to auto-email messages for an entire year, spaced out over every 3 days; others find this a bit extreme. Either way, the first week is your "hottest" period, the first month your "warmest".

As time goes on, you'll generally see your response rate drop.

Everyone has a story: what's yours?

"Story" is a hot word these days. And it should be: being able to convey the story, or the narrative, of your brand in a compelling way is a useful and impressive skill. But stories go beyond just branding alone. Understanding the structure of a story is also critical to creating a successful online business model.

Stories have a beginning, middle, and end; that's their most common characteristic. And since human beings tend to think narratively, when we discover a website and it has no beginning, middle, and end, we get a bit confused. Where should I start? Now what should I do? And after I'm done with that?

Many of the most successful-and profitable-online businesses that I know have a clear narrative structure. That is, it's obvious where the reader should begin, and where they should end up. And these businesses build their websites and products around that process.

It's what I call your Story of Engagement. Here's a good example: Bill Harris runs Centerpointe Research Institute. Its flagship technology is called Holosync®, and it has a line of products based on it. When you go to Centerpointe's website, you can see that you primarily have two options:

- Receive a demo in the mail.

- Buy Awakening Prologue.

That's important: Bill has clearly and unambiguously began his story with very few subplots. It's simple and clear to understand. Here's where it gets interesting, though: Bill has 12 other levels of his Holosync product line, each one taking the customer into a deeper level of engagement (and, as promised, bigger results). His average Customer Lifetime Value? Last I heard, it was $800. Sales? Over $16 million per year. That's an incredibly impressive feat for a personal development company.

Not everyone reading this, of course, will have only one product line that naturally lends itself to 13 levels. That's okay. I use Bill's example to demonstrate a point: making it simple for people to understand where to start, where to go next, and where to go after that-ad infinitum-not only puts them at ease, but it also increases your Customer Lifetime Value.

For example, let's say you're a leading alternative health expert and practitioner. You have a groundbreaking process for diagnosing and treating chronic symptoms that conventional doctors don't understand. You've put all of that into an information product. But you also have a series of DVDs, books, and seminars. What to do?

The art and inexact science of product laddering

What most good marketers will tell you to do is to develop a "Product Ladder": a sequence of products that people can buy over time. And, that's true. Where they sometimes confuse the universal with the viable, however, is inextricably linking price to sequence.

In other words, they'll tell you to start with the cheapest, then go more expensive, and so on. That sounds good in theory, and it can work very well. It's viable. But what if you have multiple products, and your flagship product-your best-seller, or the one you want promote most prominently-is more expensive than your other products? You don't necessarily want to start people out with the cheap ones. To go back to the Holosync example, Bill could certainly offer a cheaper product to "get people in the door." But while that may increase his on-page conversions-the number of people who buy-it may do little to help his average Value Per Visitor and average Lifetime Customer Value.

At the same time, there are marketers who do well by offering a free report; then a low-cost e-book; then a higher-priced DVD series; then a seminar; and so on. The same could be true for software: you offer a free trial, or a free account; then encourage an upgrade, and another one after that; you then introduce them to another product that complements the current one; and so on. So while Product Laddering can have a correlation to price and commitment, I wouldn't go so far as to say that it always has to; some products simply have higher barriers to entry, and that's okay.

It all depends on your market (your perfect customer), your position in the market (low-cost vs. high-cost provider), and your envisioned business structure.

How to create an online business successfully

If you want to know how to create an online business, there are a few key principles and concepts you need to understand and follow. Some of these are related directly to marketing on the internet, and some will seem somewhat removed from any type of online business venture, but are just as important nonetheless. The key elements that you need to understand are: internet business models, marketing strategies and pipelines, traffic generation techniques, and your personal motivation, vision, and value system. There are additional technical aspects to online business development and growth, but these can all be outsourced for very reasonable amounts, or even learned yourself if you can get the right information. Additionally, there are many automated tools and software that can do a lot of important tasks and jobs for you at very reasonable costs. More about that later.

There are many different types of internet business models, I will name them and define them quickly. Online businesses will flourish most completely when using as many of these strategies together as you can:

- Monetizing Adspace: This simply means getting traffic to a website, and displaying other people's ads on that site. Whenever anyone clicks on a link, whether or not they buy anything, you are paid a commission.

- Affiliate Sales: This refers to selling other people's products; generally they are information products or software.

- E-commerce: Selling physical goods online, as in an e-bay business.

- Developing your own product: Self-explanatory. Information products are a good choice here, because the cost of production is so low, allowing you to sell an almost unlimited number of copies at very low cost.

- Selling Domains: This involves buying up domains (or website names), possibly fixing the site up or even not doing anything at all, and then selling at a higher price later on.

- Online MLM: This refers to selling products through a multi-level structure, such that you are paid commissions based on sales made within your business, whether you personally referred the person who bought the product or not. This business allows for substantial residual income, and the internet has made this business model even more powerful than it was pre-internet.

- Direct Sales: Similar to MLM above, but in this case you generally are not paid commissions for sales made in a downline; or, if you are paid, it is only down one or two levels. There are some information product direct sales companies today that allow you to earn a $1,000 commission check off of just ONE sale. (Now being referred to as a Top Tier or GPT business, Get Paid Today.)

Regarding marketing strategies and pipelines, there are a few key elements that you will want to have in place. (This generally includes all online business models other than selling domains.) First, of course, is having some sort of web presence.

This can be an e-commerce store set up at yahoo stores, or your own blog. I strongly recommend having multiple locations on the web, but the heart of all of your efforts should be your own self-hosted blog.

Secondly, you should have a way of capturing people's information, so that you can market to them automatically over time. (Of course, you should offer free tremendous value to them first and foremost, and only after that market products or services to them. Or, have your offer embedded in valuable information. As an example, give away a great recipe for free, and sell them one of the main ingredients.) The preferred way here is by means of an auto-responder, which is software that can capture visitors' names and e-mails, and then send pre-written e-mails automatically to them at pre-determined intervals. Your next best option would be to have them follow you on Twitter, or subscribe to the RSS feed of your blog. Each of those ways allows you to send messages to people who are interested in hearing from you, in one form or another.

Finally, you should have a broader presence than simply your blog. You also need to be involved with some social networking sites, like Facebook, myspace, and twitter. The key is to focus on just a few of the main sites and build a presence and network of friends then. Only then should you expand out to include other sites. Just as important, you also should have as much good content as you can create, or pay to have produced in your name, on third party sites.

As far as traffic generation strategies, there really are just five sources of traffic. The trick is that there are MANY different traffic generation tactics for each source. The sources are: search engines ("organic"or free results), paid search engine traffic, social media sites, free links from other websites, and paid listings from other sites. Out of these sources, there are really three "pillars" of traffic to master: SEO (search engine optimization), PPC (refers to "pay per click" search engine ads), and social media marketing (also known as "web 2.0". Web 2.0 generally refers to websites in which users can participate in creating the content, as in posting videos to YouTube or commenting on blogs.)

I would strongly recommend mastering one of these strategies as completely as you can, depending on your goals and budget, while learning the basics of the other two. If you have a decent budget and want the quickest results, mastering PPC is the way to go. Specifically, master Google's AdWords program, since Google accounts for somewhere around 70% of search engine traffic. If you are looking for long-term significant traffic and don't have the budget for PPC, master SEO techniques (or pay someone to do it for you.) In today's internet, SEO also includes knowing some Social Media techniques. Finally, for a mix of fairly immediate traffic as well as long term potential traffic, master Social Media techniques. Just notes that the traffic generated from social media sites will not be quite as targeted as search engine traffic.

The fourth and last key element that I mentioned as necessary in creating an internet business was knowing your personal vision, motivation, and values. This may sound a little abstract, but it is just as critical as any other element. If you don't have a crystal clear image of the future results that you must have from your business, you may lose your motivation and quit. The fact is that most people who start an online business do it part-time to start with, around their main full-time job or career.

This means they have to some extent limited time to build their business, as well as other stress and responsibilities. When obstacles come up, as they surely will, they need to be smaller than your goals. If your goals are not clearly defined and at the forefront of your mind, a particularly challenging obstacle could be the thing that delivers a knock-out punch to your business plans.

Finally, having a clear idea of your core values in mind as you start your business will ensure that you choose a business you are personally interested in, and doesn't violate any of your ethical standards. If your personal ethics are compromised, or the business just isn't something you are interested in, your effort will not be 100%. And anything less than 100% commitment will put your business in serious jeopardy right from the start

Online businesses and their overlooked top secret weapon

One of the main concerns of any Internet Marketer today resides in driving targeted and quality traffic to their business or product website on a daily basis. There are lots of ways through which they can achieve that, but most entrepreneurs will agree on the fact that having a professional and effective squeeze page is the starting point to building their prospects list exponentially. A Squeeze page or landing page, as it is called by some people, is a single web page with the sole purpose of capturing information for follow-up marketing, to finally create a large client list. Although it seems like a simple thing, where interested people will basically input their name and email address in fields provided on that page, it should contain a few key characteristics in order to work properly:

- **A big, attention-grabbing logo** - take a look at Google, eBay, Yahoo and all the other web giants today, and the first thing you'll find on their pages is a BIG, colored logo right in the middle of the website on a white background. That same principle should apply to your squeeze page. It has been proven that graphic elements, specially a trustworthy logo, will inspire customers to share their contact information with businesses and their offers. It is not a mandatory thing to follow though, since there are lots of color schemes and design templates that are just as effective, as long as they are planned correctly.

- **Oversized and well design buttons** - top online businesses have to make it clear to possible clients that they want them to take a specific action, which is to input their information in the submission form at the lower part of the webpage. An oversized well designed Submit button is eye catching and will send that message clearly to the visitor and his or her subconscious. So start thinking BIG.

- **Use audio and video** - statistics show that there is a 300% increase in the conversion rate of browsers into buyers, when Internet marketers make use of video and audio resources on their squeeze page. When done in a professional way, you will be enticing the use of the visual and auditive senses, which makes a gigantic difference to the number of people that will finally join your list and possibly purchase a product from you.

- **Concise and convincing title** - it is no secret that when a squeeze page has an exciting title or headline, visitors are driven to read through the rest of the information and are naturally taken to the lower portion of the page where the graphically interesting input field is. And this is the whole point of having a landing page. So be informative, concise and creative with your headline. Clearly state your unique selling proposition here.

The second part of the overlooked top secret weapon of businesses today, which are capture pages, is called the Sales Letter. Just as the name implies, this is where you actually describe the service or product you market, and finally develop a pleasant, natural and creative sales pitch. It should contain specific information regarding what users signed up for and its benefits. And that is crucial! Because useless information will most likely distract users, causing them to lose interest and click-away to a different site.

The sales letter, just like your Squeeze Page, should always detail what the subscriber will be receiving and describe the privacy standards offered by the company to avoid their fear of spam. Always include a privacy disclaimer right beneath your submission form. Also, make sure to present visitors with multiple BUY NOW links consistently throughout the page; it is recommended to have at least 10 of these links in total. Remember that users might read something as they go down the page that may cause them to buy a product right away, so always have a BUY NOW link nearby.

After sorting the Sales Letter, you will need a professional Auto Responder service. And what that is basically, is a series of automated messages sent to each user that submitted their information to your business and became a subscriber to your service, with the sole purpose of convincing prospects of the advantages of the products you offer and finally generate sales. There is an excellent option when it comes to auto responders called aWebber. Google it up. There are specific tutorials on their site, explaining what it is and how to set it up and get it up and running with your business right away.

Keep in mind that when sending messages via auto-responders, try to reach your prospects on a daily basis, or every 2 days. If you write them well you will definitely stay away from the spammer tag. That way, the excitement of your offer will always remain fresh and they will be reminded each day of why they chose to be part of your list. Write smart messages, avoid spam and ALWAYS link back to your sales site.

The last part of this secret process is the Thank You page. It is a webpage designed to express how valuable your clients are to your business by simply saying thank you and goodbye in a professional manner. This builds credibility for your business and loyalty on their end, giving them the importance they deserve. Remember, the most important part of marketing and any business model known to man, are customers.

So here is an overview of the exact steps in using the secret weapon that is a professional sale process starting with an effective squeeze page:

- A well designed Squeeze Page or Landing Page

- An informative and convincing Sales Letter

- A professional auto-responder service

- A friendly thank you or goodbye page

As a final note, this structure will apply to every single online business model, since this system has been tested over and over again by many successful marketers around the world. It does not take a long time surfing on the Internet to realize that 90% of businesses that are actually generating profit to their owners work this way, because it is an affordable and organized way of building an extensive client list.

That is exactly what it takes for you to start achieving the same success right away. Do things right once and you will enjoy quality traffic and a big number of sales on autopilot forever.

Most common mistakes of starting online business

Why your success online has nothing to do with building a website. Most entrepreneurs starting online make the flawed assumption that starting a business on the internet is about building a websites, creating a product and traffic will follow. This is far from the truth. The truth is that your success in business online has more to do than building a website. The truth is...the internet is a medium for doing business, you still need to build a real business that provides value to your customers and serves your market.

You need to understand that business is the most important game you will ever play... because you spend more time, energy and money on your business than you'll ever spend elsewhere. And this is the reasons you must avoid the mistakes most entrepreneurs make online. So you can grow your business and start to live the life you always wanted.
Here are some of the mistakes businesses make online....

Mistake 1: Coming up with a great idea

Many entrepreneurs make the mistake of thinking their idea is the next big thing to hit the market. There is nothing wrong in coming up with ideas for a product; however, you must ensure that your idea for a product will serve to solve a problem in your niche.

Solution
Come up with great ideas that will serve the wants and needs of an existing market

Mistake 2: Create a product

This faulty assumption relies on the idea that people will come knocking at your door if you build a better widget. This is far from the truth, because there are millions of products competing for your consumers' attention.

Solution

What you need is to identify your market -a group of people with interest and desire for your product, willing to spend money. Then you provide them a better or unique way to enjoy what they already want.Steve Jobs (Apple)created a completely new experience for the customer first with the iPod, then iphone and now the ipad. The same example you can find with Amazon.com; the company changed the buying experience for the consumer online.

Mistake 3: Selling with logic

Most people make buying decisions on emotions. The typical buyer will buy what appeals to their core desires. It is very important to understand what your customer wants from your product when you are creating the product and marketing it. You product must appeal to your customer's want

Solution

Always think about the benefit of your product for your customers, and then sell him these benefits.

Mistake 4: Choosing the wrong market

Another common mistake many businesses make is selling their product to the wrong market- the right message to the wrong audience. Let me explain. For instance, you cannot be selling baby products to single people, unless they are thinking of starting families. In the same vein, you will not succeed if you want to sell single family homes to a single person who is not yet ready to settle down to start a family. Yet, this is what most marketers do... selling to the wrong crowd.

Solution

Research and find your market, see what type of marketing promotions they are responding to, listen to their frustrations and solve their problems

Mistake 5: Being opportunistic instead of being strategic

Opportunity seekers are a group of people who are always looking for the next money making ideas. They tend to chase after the next hot trends and never really settle down to build real businesses.

This kind of mindset is present in most business starting out online. I am not against making money, however if the basis of starting a business is just to make money, and not to serve the customer then you destined to fail.

On the other hand, if you start your business with a focus to serve your market, deliver outstanding products and service then you stand a better chance to succeed online.In addition,when you experience the initial difficulties most start-up businesses face- you see this as part of the learning curve in your entrepreneurial adventure-and will not give up.

Solution

Be strategic. Have a clear vision and purpose for starting your business. Take time to study and know your customers and market you serve. If you have this kind of mindset then you will have an unfair advantage over your competition.

Mistake 6: Lack of knowledge and skills

According to SCORE(the service core of retired executives), an advisory arm of the the U.S Small Business administration of America SBA, one of the major reasons small businesses fail is lack of knowledge and business skills on the part of the owners of the business. The sad reality is this cause also applies to small businesses online.

Majority of entrepreneurs buy generic websites, sell products they have no knowledge of and are not passionate. The result is failure to attract customers and business failure. The internet is a channel for doing business...Just because it's easy to set up a website, set up landing pages, hire copy writers to write sales letters for you does not mean you can get away with anything. Internet users are sophisticated and can tell when you don't understand or know your product.

Solution

You need to be in a business you know something about. Even if you don't have a passion for the niche you have choose, you can read, research and reflect.

The other option is to look for experts in the area of business you are involved and form partnerships with them. Remember you want to build your reputation and your company needs to have integrity.

Mistake 7: Not building a relationship with your customers

There is an axiom in internet marketing that says, "The money is in your list". This means your continued survival and sales as a business depend on having a I relationship with a base of customers, who spend money on your products on a recurring basis.

The mistake most entrepreneurs make is that they focus on making sales. Brian Tracy, bestselling author "Psychology of Selling" says the primary aim of your business is to acquire customers.

Here is why: It is easier to sell to someone who has bought from you than a prospect. The other obvious reason is if you delight your customers, you can sell more of the products they want.

There is a concept in marketing called the Lifetime value LTV of a customer. This means your customers, have a net cash value from the time the transact business with you. If you are focused on only making a sale then you will not be able to take advantage of the LTV of your customers.

Your first sale that is hard, as long as you satisfy your customer subsequent sales is easy.

Solution

focus on building a list of customers. develop good follow up and customer service systems. Let me drive home the importance of this point by ending with what Mary Ellen-Tribby, expert marketer and bestselling author Changing the Channels: 12 Easy Ways to make money for your business says if you don't have a list of customers, you are running a garage sale.

Mistake 8: Not working with a proven business model

Another common mistake, most entrepreneurs make on line is not working with a proven business model for their businesses.By not having a proven business model, youare bound to fail.

Why use a proven business model? Proven models work and deliver profits to your business. There are many proven business models online. Your job is to find the one that is best match for your business

Solution
Don't try to reinvent the wheel. find and work with proven business models. If you can avoid these common mistakes, most entrepreneurs make you will stack the odds in your favour to grow your business and begin to live the life you always wanted to live.

How you can share in Amazon's global success

Amazon is the sales marketplace that originally started out as a place to sell books. But in the last decade it's graduated to selling anything and everything... and become one of the biggest brands in the world. Not only that but it's a famous brand that allows - in fact encourages - entrepreneurs to share in their success by selling products right there on Amazon itself. Over the last couple of years Amazon have been working on another way you can make money in partnership with them. It's called Fulfillment by Amazon (FBA).

Now to me Fulfillment by Amazon sounds like a really exciting way of making money in the 21st century Internet age. Because it is a business model whereby you can just focus on marketing and making sales. Then have Amazon do all the "hard" physical work of stocking, storing and shipping your products to your customers for you.

You know, Amazon are always something of a puzzle to me! They come out with the latest, cutting-edge business models and invest millions in making them successful. There's no doubt Amazon's brand image, ordering and distribution systems are absolutely without equal. Then they let any Tom, Dick or Harriet share them for free. Just why they would let ordinary people take advantage of all this for no up-front cost whatsoever, I don't know! It seems crazy, it doesn't seem to make sense at all, but they do it... and it's almost always a big success.

So I thought it's high time we came back to Amazon and looked at exactly how Fulfillment by Amazon works, whether it is as good as it sounds... and whether it can make some money for you.

... did you know?

- Amazon attracts 50 million consumers a month worldwide.

- Amazon has been voted the third favourite UK retailer (after John Lewis and IKEA).

- 1.3 million businesses are selling on Amazon.

- Amazon's business grew 18% last year... when most businesses were shrinking.

So, what is Fulfillment by Amazon exactly?

The basic concept of Fulfillment by Amazon, like all Amazon's concepts, is simple... although there are a lot of ins-and-outs which I'll look at later. With this service you send whatever products you want to sell (your inventory as Amazon like to call it) directly to Amazon.

Whether it be books, CDs, clothing, computer accessories, toys, or whatever. They store it in their warehouse for you. Then when orders are received Amazon will pick, pack and ship the product directly to your customers for you.

You can use Fulfillment by Amazon whether you just want to sell a few things on Amazon as a sideline or want to sell thousands of products. You can use it if you are starting a new business or have an existing one that you want to change over to Fulfillment by Amazon. You can use Fulfillment by Amazon to send out things you are selling on Amazon itself or things you are selling elsewhere. This is what Amazon called Multi Channel Fulfillment. One more thing: if you start using Fulfillment by Amazon you don't have to have everything fulfilled by Amazon. You can use it for some products and not others.

Pros and cons

So then, let's have a look at the pros and cons of Fulfillment by Amazon:

Pros

I.   You get to benefit from Amazon's reputation. Amazon is a brand that's trusted by customers worldwide. When they order something that is shipped by Amazon they know they will get it. And fast. And they know they can return it if they want to. This can make a massive difference when they are deciding whether to buy from you.

II.   You can offer faster service. Amazon has state-of-the-art online order processing and fulfillment operations. Chances are they can get your products to your buyers faster than you can.

III.   Your products can be ranked higher on Amazon. With an Fulfillment by Amazon item your item shows up at the top of the search more often than not. Products from non- Fulfillment by Amazon sellers are listed by total cost (product price plus shipping) but your items are listed by price only. So often you can price your items close to the lowest total price, maybe be the first item in the list and attract more buyers.

IV.   Your customers can get free delivery. Using Fulfillment by Amazon will mean your customers get free delivery on your products... using Super Saver Delivery or Amazon Prime. That can give you a big advantage over sellers who don't use Fulfillment by Amazon.

V.   Lower overheads. You'll need to do the figures but, in most cases, there can be good cost savings. With FBA you won't need premises for storage, staff to do picking/shipping and associated admin. It might even mean you can drop your prices, sell more goods and yet still make more profit.

VI.   You can be MUCH more productive. I think this is the biggest potential benefit. When you use FBA you won't need to spend time sorting, warehousing, picking and packing goods. Amazon do it for you. They can also handle customer services, returns, etc.
This means you can spend almost all your time actually marketing and selling - things that make you money. And because you can spend more time doing that you should, at least in theory, be able to make more money.

Now, although Amazon will tell you there aren't any disadvantages to FBA I think there are a few you need to bear in mind:

Cons

I.   It's not so good for products that take a long time to sell or which are unproven sellers. Because you have to pay a monthly storage fee for as long as Amazon have your products.

II.   Using FBA might make it difficult to compete with other sellers, especially those also using FBA. Because how are you going to differentiate your product and your service from theirs?

III.   This is what I think is the main drawback of Fulfillment by Amazon. Your business is almost totally reliant on Amazon.
What if something goes wrong... for example their systems fail and they don't fulfill your orders or lose your stock? Or if they put up their prices?

Getting started with fulfillment by Amazon

So let's have a look at how you can get started using Fulfillment by Amazon.

At this point I should say that there's tons of detailed information on how it all works at the Amazon website. But that's really hard going and a lot of it is difficult to follow. So here I'm going to try to give you a simple, user-friendly summary of Fulfillment by Amazon.

First of all Fulfillment by Amazon is not separate to the other methods of using Amazon. It is fully integrated with them. You just set up to sell on Amazon Marketplace in the usual way then choose to FBA the products you want to.

It's very easy to get started with Amazon Marketplace. You don't need to register in advance. You can open a seller account when you list your first product. To register as a seller you will need a business name, an address, a display name (which can be your business name or something else), a credit card and a telephone contact number. That's all you need to get started. Go to http://www.amazon.co.uk, scroll down the page to 'Make Money With Us' and then 'Sell On Amazon' to get started.

Amazon offers two ways of selling - informally called 'selling a little' or 'selling a lot'. Basically 'a little' is for occasional and hobby sellers who expect to sell less than 35 items a month. It costs 86p plus a referral fee for each sale and you can't sell in all the Amazon categories. Selling 'a lot' is for businesses who expect to sell more than 35 items a month. You pay a £28.75 monthly fixed fee and a referral fee. You can sell in all the Amazon product categories. The 'selling a little' option isn't really for use with Fulfillment by Amazon.

To use Fulfillment by Amazon fully you will also really need to become what Amazon call a Pro Merchant Seller. Pro Merchants have access to volume selling and bulk listing tools. There is a web interface that allows you to more easily manage your product descriptions, inventory and orders. You will also be able to export and import information to and from your account. Normally the Pro Merchant option will work out much cheaper and therefore will allow you to work on tighter margins and make money from products and sales those who sell just "a little" can't.

If you are already selling on Amazon all you need to do is convert to a business account and ask them to enrol you in Fulfillment by Amazon. It doesn't cost anything to sign up so you can just try it and see how you get on.

Valuable Tip

When you sign up to Fulfilment by Amazon with Amazon.co.uk you can only sell things within the UK. Which strikes me as a bit odd, seeing as how the Internet is supposed to be a global way of doing business. You can sell using Fulfillment by Amazon in some of the other countries Amazon operates in - Germany, France, USA and Japan - but you need to sign up with them separately. Initially you probably wouldn't want to do this but it could be a way of expanding in future.

Sales example: sell used books working from home

Getting started selling in the Amazon Marketplace is easy. You probably already have most of these items on hand already. If money is tight, buy small quantities to get started (envelopes, tape, bubble wrap for shipping) to help economize during your start-up phase. Later on you can buy in bulk and save money. You will need:

- A computer with Internet access - If you're reading this you likely already have your own computer. You'll need it every day for researching book prices, list books for sale, and check for email notifications.

- Shipping envelopes - Large brown manila envelopes sized 9" x 12" and 10" x 13" work really well to ship most books.

- Bubble wrap - Protects the books from damage in mail. You can buy a small roll of clear bubble wrap these days at many discount stores for about $5 to get started. This will save you money vs. buying bubble wrap envelopes and help you ship items that you might wind up selling on eBay or on other online sellers websites.

- USPS Confirmation Delivery slips - These are available free from your local Post Office. They are the green and white slips that have a peel-and-stick adhesive at one end. Ask for a stack of 50-100 to get started.

- Black ink pens - Have plenty on hand for addressing packages, Delivery Confirmation slips, shipping labels and making notes for yourself.

- Pencils with erasers - Many libraries and some thrift shops will go through the process of marking the inside front cover with a price in pencil before their sale gets started.

This price is usually $1, $2, $3 - and you'll need to erase this evidence that you got a terrific steal on this book when you're selling it for 10 times what you paid for it!

- Scissors - For trimming up mis-taped parcels and cutting down cardboard packing protectors for supporting thin booklets or paperbacks. Also, you'll need these to cut up the bubblewrap you will use to protect books during shipment.

- File folders - Use up some old manila file folders you were going to get rid of anyway if you don't want to buy new ones, which cost about $5 for a small package. Trim these into two pieces, one to protect front of book and one to protect back cover of book, once you slide the book into the shipping envelope to provide extra protection to your parcel.

- Clear heavy-duty shipping tape & tape gun - You'll need the tape gun and 2-3 rolls of clear tape to get started. You can buy the smaller plastic tape dispensers for about $3 each if you're short on cash.

- Cleaning supplies- You probably already have these in your kitchen: paper towels, small clean brush, warm water. Don't use cleaning sprays to remove stains from books or the dust covers. Most times you can put a small amount of warm water on a paper towel, swipe it across the glossy dust covers, and restore a clean shine to the book dust cover.

- Bookshelves - Needless to say, this business inventory tends to take up lots of room, so set aside a spare bedroom or a cool, dry place in your home that has low humidity, away from windows that sweat to prevent damage to the paper in the books, and invest in or build some shelving to hold your books.

- Work Table - Yes, you can use your dining room table, but having a designated work table like a long folding table that can be stowed away in a utility closet is a nice way to get an assembly line going for (a) listing books and (2) packing books for shipment.

- Mobile Smartphone - OK, I'll admit that this is optional. Most cellphone smartphones will take a big chunk out of your monthly budget. But when you use the phone's internet web browser while out shopping to pull up competing prices, you'll know for certain if you've found a winner or not within seconds, so there's no second guessing.

- Account Set-Up - You will need a business checking account to have payments direct deposited into from your book sales. Ask at your bank for a free debit card to go with account, and you won't need to write many checks out of this account. You can use the debit card to make the purchases you'll need to start and operate your bookselling business.

Other business needs are:

- You will need a credit card (attention: debit card is not accepted!) - You will need one for Amazon to confirm your sellers account the day you get started (it doesn't get charged again after that).

- You will need a phone number - Home number or cell phone number that Amazon will use to send you a confirmation call or text message to confirm your identity when setting up account (this phone number doesn't get published on your online storefront unless you want to put it there - and I'd recommend against that. Your customers need to contact you via email anyway).

- You will need a valid email address - This is where you'll send messages and receive book sale notifications and to check email notices regarding returns. I'd recommend getting a new Gmail account, and keep your business and your private email accounts separate.

- Check with your city zoning department - While it boggles my mind that some cities restrict home businesses, it happens. You may need a business license in your town. You won't have customers or supplier sales reps coming to your home, and unless you're having UPS pick up large quantities of your books to ship to the nearest 'Fulfilled By Amazon' (FBA) distribution center, your neighbors probably will never notice you even run a home based business unless you tell them.

Now that you know the essential items you'll need to get started selling used books on Amazon, it's time to get busy sourcing books to sell online. It's easy to make money when you stock up on the right kinds of books. Take your time, negotiate for the best prices, and limit your purchases to good condition books. Your home based book store will take time to get up and running, but having the right tools handy starting out will help you get more done in less time as you learn how to sell in the Amazon Marketplace!

E-commerce: selling online by yourself

In today's world, where technology reigns, people have become extremely dependent on the internet. They communicate online, work online, conduct research projects online, and spend their money online. For a business that wants to succeed in the electronic age, it is often necessary to jump on the bandwagon and set up shop online. This article contains a quick overview of e-commerce and how to effectively market a business on the internet.

What is e-commerce? Simply put, it is the buying and selling of products online. There are several key elements to e-commerce that you will need to start selling online:

- Website, Web Design and Hosting

- Marketing

- Online Payment Processors

- Suppliers and Drop Shippers

Website, Web Design and Hosting

Selling online is impossible without a website. Through this website, consumers are introduced to your product, allowed to browse through what you have available, and then purchase a product and have their order delivered to their door. While all this sounds easy, there is a lot of work behind the scenes to get a website up and running.

The first thing you will need is a good computer. Although you probably won't be doing the web design yourself, you will need to have access to your website to track visitors and purchases, as well as receive orders. If you can't access your store via your computer it's a little like being locked out of your shop without the front door key. You will also need another computer to actually host the website, as well as handle financial transactions but there are 100's of hosting companies out there and you can rent a web server for as little as £20 per month for this purpose.

Your website, and the way it is designed is perhaps the number one thing that affects sales. No one wants to buy from a website that opens slowly, is not aesthetically pleasing, is difficult to browse through, and involves too many steps to purchase the product. Buyers will quickly head to another website. Start out by making sure your website presents a good face, with well-chosen colors, good graphics (although there should not be too many, as graphics slow down the opening of the webpage) and clear, easy to find categories and options. It is important to divide your products logically, creating 'shelves' or categories in your online store. Having to search too hard for a specific product is a turn-off to most customers. You will also need to include a small amount of text with each product, giving all pertinent information about it.

When it comes time to purchase, convenience is key. All websites today include a 'shopping cart', where consumers can place items they wish to order while they continue browsing. This is conducive to making more sales, as the customer can buy several items at once, instead of having to purchase one at a time. Payment options are another important aspect of your purchasing system.

To get your website online, you need a host. A web host is a company that owns or leases a server on which they provide space for your website, in addition to furnishing internet connectivity. There are a wide variety of web hosts, all of whom provide different levels of benefits. For an e-commerce site, a slightly more advanced web host is necessary to allow for financial transactions, etc. There are some free web hosts, but most require a monthly or yearly payment.

Finally, make sure your website has a good domain name. Keep it short and simple, making it easy to remember. Try to tie it in with your products, keeping in mind your clientele.

Marketing

A great website doesn't make sales alone. You need to market your website, and one of the best ways to do so is with search engine optimization. Making sure your website appears near the top of a web search can get you a lot of new buyers. Your web designer can help with this, or there are several free guides online that offer tips. Pay per click advertising is another great form of marketing that will get you instant results.

These are the ads you see appear on the search engines in the right hand column and occasionally at the top of the results pages. This can be costly but can also reap great rewards if done well and your web designer should be able to help in this area also.

Don't forget offline marketing methods when running an e-commerce business. Although your site is online your potential customers are not glued to their computers all day. They still read magazines and newspapers, look at billboards and various other media we're subjected to every day. If your website address is short and snappy it will stick in their mind and you can effectively advertise anywhere to get new business.

Payment Processors

To complete financial transactions on your website, you will need a payment processor. A payment processor is a company that you designate to handle your credit card transactions. This company takes the details of the credit card being offered and authorizes its use for making a purchase.

It then places the payment in a merchant account, which is an account specifically designed for accepting these payments. It also acts as an agreement between you (the merchant), your bank and your payment processor. Once again, there are many payment processors which provide different services with varied fees. Some include a built in merchant account, while others do not. It is important to research this subject thoroughly, as a bad payment processor can be a major headache and cost you money.

The best place to start when looking at payment processing online is your bank. You will need a merchant account with them and it's usually not worth shopping around as they all seem to be of a similar price. It's basically just another account that holds the funds before depositing into your business bank account. The payment processor however is another story. The fees from these companies vary quite dramatically and it's advisable to look into 2 or 3 to get an idea of current prices. Sage Pay is one of the most popular at present as they offer a flat monthly fee for a set number of transactions each month which makes their service one of the best value at the moment.

Suppliers and Drop Shippers

Unless you make your product yourself, you will usually purchase products from a supplier at wholesale, and then resell the product at retail price. When selling products online, the need for having the item in stock at your physical store may not be necessary. Often however a buyers decision will be made on the premise that they can get the item quickly. People shopping online today expect an item to arrive quickly unless it is clearly stated on the website. Many online companies choose to use the drop shipping services provided by a number of wholesalers. Instead of ordering the product, repackaging it and mailing it to the customer, they have the product shipped directly to the customer from the supplier's site. This system saves both time and money, as it cuts back on labor costs and improves efficiency. However, a possible downside to the drop shipping method is back orders. There may be times a purchase is made, but you discover the supplier is out of stock. Keeping in close contact with your supplier can minimize these types of problems.

Participating in e-commerce can be challenging, but it may be just what you need to take your company to the next level in business today.

Drop-shipping versus affiliate marketing: which is better?

For someone making a debut in e-commerce, drop-shipping, affiliate marketing, and wholesaling are a plethora of terms that may leave you perplexed and looking for answers as to which is the safest and most lucrative career move.

In drop-shipping, buyers buy items that you can sell either in online stores or through eBay and that are thereafter supplied from warehouses belonging to your supplier. What is most vital here is getting a trustworthy and efficient supplier who will handle all inventory issues and shipping concerns. Extracting money for those items from your buyer is your only concern when you opt for drop-shipping. However, in affiliate marketing, the actual effort that you need to put in is even less than in drop-shipping. If you can ensure search engine optimization and advertisements for your portal, you can still churn in huge profits even when you have no direct involvement.

The basic idea for both business models is to sell items that you do not need to stock or buy, and when you get a client, the item is shipped directly.

So long as getting customers comes easily to you, both these business options are equally profitable. But, drop-shipping apparently has some advantages over affiliate marketing.

1. In drop-shipping, you have the liberty of getting your own customers and building your own clientele, whom you can regularly contact time and again whenever you have potentially interesting products to offer them. In affiliate marketing, the focus is exclusively on making money and not so much on networking that can, in turn, promote your business even further. This is possibly why many of those who started off as investors in affiliate marketing are now toying with the idea of drop-shipping.

2. Drop-shipping calls for more commitment and responsibility because you are answerable for late deliveries or defective products. This, however, gives a drop-shipping business the freedom to negotiate on price quotes and contracts with suppliers; that means greater gains. In affiliate marketing, the degree of flexibility is considerably limited, and you must follow the clauses in the merchant's agreement. The only means of making greater profits through commissions is by ensuring greater sales. The positive side is that you do not need to be hassled with customer service concerns, which are completely handled by the merchants in question.

3. When your aim is to establish a real business, drop-shipping is the preferred alternative. This alone can give you greater control over price negotiations and your clients, most importantly. Affiliate marketing involves less effort and time in getting good suppliers because you can start selling simply by joining any of the multiple affiliate schemes available. The modus operandi is simple, but control is automatically restricted.

4. Drop-shipping allows you to decide on the price of a product, but in affiliate marketing, you must sell it at the price quoted by the merchant. So, drop-shipping can be competitive where there are many sellers, but this is not possible in affiliate marketing, where the only way to better profit margins is by maintaining low costs.

Both drop-shipping and affiliate marketing are excellent means of doing online business and making money without the hassles of being stuck with loads of unsold products and paying for the inventory. The whole idea is to have a steady source of income that requires minimum investment.

Using drop shipping for e-commerce

Thanks to the ubiquity of the internet, online virtual businesses have become very popular business opportunities. Online retail stores are gradually playing a more important role in our lives than the traditional 'brick-and-mortar' retail shops. Over the last few years, a new concept called 'Drop Shipping' has emerged with the coming of the internet. Drop Shippers are basically wholesalers who are willing to ship their products directly to your customers. This article aims to provide readers with an introduction to the current state of the E-commerce industry, Drop Shipping and its benefits, and the promise it holds for the online retail community.

Online Drop Ship businesses are now very popular home-based business opportunities. According to a Forrester Inc. report, online retail sales will grow at a 25% annual growth rate over the next five years. Online retail sales will reach nearly $230 billion and account for 10% of total US retail sales by 2008. On Ebay, more than 430,000 people are making a full- or part-time living from the auction site.

Many of them use Drop Shippers to auction their products. Hence, with such strong statistics, the internet entrepreneur can hope to start a retail business now and still claim a portion of the ever-growing market share.

The Drop Ship model offers many unique advantages over the Wholesale model:

1) You do not have to spend a fortune on the huge inventory of wholesale stocks before you start a retail business. This translates into a very low business startup cost. There is no risk of purchasing large quantities of stock, and finding that you cannot sell off your goods because they have become obsolete among consumers. Therefore, with the variety of products offered by your Drop Shipper, it becomes feasible to test which products have a

strong demand over the internet without losing a fortune on each test.

2) Another prime advantage of a Drop Ship business is that there is no need to worry about shipping your products to your customers. You do not have to provide storage space for your goods, nor do you have to incur warehouse costs. Your Drop Shipper will take care of all the logistics and shipping of your Drop Ship business. In fact, most Drop Shippers are willing to label their products with your company name on it, so it will appear as if you are the one who shipped the products to your customers. The shipping cost for each product is also reduced, because your Drop Shipper can ship your products directly to your customers. A higher profit margin is achieved because of the reduction in unnecessary shipping costs.

3) Drop Shipping is also unique in that it allows you to 'sell high, then buy low', instead of 'buy low, then sell high'. Your risk involved in your retail business is dramatically lowered as you get paid up front for your products, making a profit on each sale.

4) There is no minimum quantity restriction on your orders. From your website catalogue, you can sell as much of your products as you want, and you can leave the indenting of stocks to your Drop Shipper. The quantity of products which you can sell over your website is only limited to your market demand, and your marketing efforts.

The process of setting up a Drop Ship business can be distilled into a few simple steps. First, you do some research over the internet over the niche market that you would like to target. Once, a strong demand for your products has been established, you contact the Drop Shipper of your choice and set up your business as the retailer of the products you want to sell. Next, you design a website complete with product catalogue and credit-card-accepting functions. The product descriptions and images can be obtained from the Drop Shipper, in most cases. After which, you need to drive large volumes of traffic to your website through internet marketing. Some visitors to your website will be converted to customers if they find your offers attractive enough. They place orders at your website and they pay you the retail prices, up front. You email the orders to your Drop Shipper, who will ship the products to your customers directly. Of course, the retail price will have to be marked up to include shipping costs as well. Since the Drop Shipper charges you the wholesale price for their products, the profit margin you earn is simply the difference between the retail and wholesale price.

In conclusion, the e-commerce industry is still very promising despite the dot-com bust a few years back. With the introduction of Drop Shipping, the hassles of conducting a retail business over the internet have been dramatically reduced. As the industry is still relatively young, entrepreneurs should get in the e-commerce game early to establish themselves as strong market players of the future.

Make money by YouTube

How to make a YouTube video - and how to drive traffic to it.

Have you ever wanted to show yourself to the world? Have you ever wanted the rest of the world to see what you look like and how you speak, and as if you're directly talking to them? Would you like to feel famous and well known? Maybe you would like to share your opinion on something or to provide information to the world.

You can, on a website called YouTube! And it's easy too!

Step 1 - Getting the right video editing software (optional)

If you'd like to communicate your message more efficiently on YouTube, I recommend that you purchase a video-editing software. Yes, you can take a "selfie" video of yourself on your smartphone and then upload it to YouTube for free, but your video may be a little shaky and garbled at times. Besides, a lot of these software applications make it very easy to upload your video to YouTube. Plus, you can also use the software to create some special effects for your video.

Prices for the software can be anywhere from $30 - $200 or more. There's also "FREE" software that you can download, but be warned; most free software has extreme limitations on what you can do. If you're unsure of what software to buy, I recommend that you go to your nearest computer store such as "Best Buys", and ask one of the workers there which software they think is the best. You can also go to "Google" and type in "Best Video-editing software" and see what you find.

Once you do get your software DVD, just insert the DVD into the DVD player and the program should easily walk you through. Or if you download the software, just follow the directions and you'll be fine.

Well done! You're on your way to making videos!

Step 2- Buying a Webcam

A webcam is a device that lets you record yourself, and also communicate with other people online. But webcams can also record videos that you can then store onto your computer. Furthermore, webcams are great for a better video, because you can put your webcam right on top of your computer monitor, and then record your video while you sit down comfortably. This will allow you to present a less shaky and more stable video.

Of course, you can still take videos with a smartphone or a video camcorder, and for some types of videos, it could be useful, such as recording a video of a child's birthday party.

However with a webcam, You won't need to worry about a shaky camera, and your message should be clear. Additionally, webcams are usually inexpensive. As with I mentioned earlier about buying the right video editing software, do the same thing for webcams. Talk to your local computer store worker. They'll help you out. Of course, once again you can "Google" for the right webcam.

Installing your webcam is quite easy too. If you need more help, you can always ask a computer store worker for better directions, or there should be a customer support phone number on the webcam's package. All it usually takes is plugging the Webcam into the computer, and then installing the software.

Step 3 - Explore and get familiar with your new software and Webcam. Have fun!

All righty then! You've spent a fair amount of time and money getting your video editing software and webcam, so now it's time for you to take a break and have some fun! You've earned it! Play around with your webcam and video software and learn about it. Get familiar with it until it becomes almost second nature. Learn a few tricks about inserting some crazy special effects on your video. But really, Have fun doing all of this. You'll probably learn better when you're more relaxed.

And if you need help or have a question about anything, there's usually a "Help" section for the software or you can always call customer support. Once you feel that you've mastered your webcam and software, it's time for the next step.

Step 4 - Explore and get familiar with YouTube. Have some more fun!

You've probably done this I'm sure. In this day and age, almost everybody who has a computer and online access has gone on YouTube to look at videos. Watching videos on YouTube is as common as emailing or googling.

There's a lot of videos of ordinary people like you and me, just doing everyday things, such as: watering a plant or playing with their pets. Or just talking about something. Explore YouTube and watch other peoples' videos. This may give you an idea of what kind of video you'd like to create.

Step 5 - Deciding on what kind of video you want to make

Perhaps you want to give your opinion on politics. Or maybe you'd like to talk about a certain movie. On the other hand, maybe you would like to show the world how well trained your German Shepard is. if you feel that you have an important message and would like to clearly communicate with your audience, you may just want to write a script for yourself. Just write down what you'd like to say, and then record your video, using your script as a guide.
Why not? It just might make your presentation more clear and focused

Step 6 - Filming your "serious" video

Once you've gotten your idea nailed down and have a great way of presenting it, just record your video and label that video as one of the "IMPORTANT " ones. This video will show your image to the world after all.

How to set up your YouTube videos

So you are ready to use YouTube. You have all these fantastic videos that you are ready to share with the cyber world, but what is the next step? First and foremost, you want to visit YouTube.com. This is YouTube's website. On the top right corner there is a link titled "Create Account". Follow the steps to create your account and then you will be ready to share away with your videos.

Before attempting to post your videos, remember that there are some requirements each video has to follow in order to be posted on YouTube. The majority of the time, this will not be a problem, with the most important guideline being that the video has to remain under 10 minutes.

There are also file size requirements (100MB or less). The following is a beginners guide to uploading a video onto YouTube:

- Very first thing you have to do to upload a video is click the "Upload Videos" link. These are located on the top right of the page and are on almost every page on YouTube.

- Next you are going to be asked to briefly describe your video. You will first need to enter a title and a description for your video. Keep these simple as people are not going to want to read a long description (they are on a video watching site, not an E-Book site). After the description section there is an area to enter tags for your video. Tags are keywords that will help your video be found based off what the user is searching for. You are going to want to use important words for this section.

- Following the tags section you will have to select a category and language to place your video in. It is important to select the correct category and language, as this will also help your video be found to users who are looking for that specific type of content. Finally, click "Go Upload A File".

The next page asks if you would like your video to be available to the public, or private. If you are wanting to get your business name out there, you will want to keep this public as this allows the millions of visitors the opportunity to view your video. Next click, "Upload Video". This will bring you to a page to browse your computer for the video you wish to upload. After finding the video, select it and your video will be live within minutes.

Get people to see the video

The video you just uploaded is a hidden gem among the sea of the internet. Next, we need to get people to find this gem. One very basic way to get people to view your video is to create a link on your business website to your YouTube video, or have your YouTube video embedded on your site itself. With that said, you can also link to any sites (business or social networks) that your business is linked with. Just remember, the more exposure to the video, the better. One great tactic that many businesses use is promoting some sort of contest through their YouTube account. The draw of winning something will bring in more viewers.

YouTube also allows users many great ways to get people to your video. When you initially signed up for YouTube, you created a channel. In other words, if you signed up as "Business 1", there is now a "Business 1 Channel" on YouTube. Having your own channel allows you to create your own playlists. This playlist can consist of videos you upload or videos others have uploaded that you have viewed and want to share with others. Sharing someone else's video may in turn entice them to share your video.

On the same note, underneath all videos (unless this option is turned off) there is a section for commenting. Commenting on other videos is a great tool to promote your business. Keep in mind, this DOES NOT mean to comment on someone's video "Check out my video...". This is spam, and will most likely be deleted. What you want to do is comment on a users video that is related to the topic of your video. Also, you want to keep the comments relevant and not so generic. A comment like "cool video", "'nice job", etc. will not gain you any attention. A comment that is more conversational shows the author that you are paying attention throughout their video as well as reading the comments.

This will possibly strike their interest in clicking your username, and therefore being brought to your channel to view your videos. The more you do this, the better the opportunity of getting numerous views is.

There are also the following options on YouTube to help get your video out there: emails/messages, bulletins, chat, and rating. These will help because you will be emailing, posting, and chatting on related topics will prove to be useful because you can get someone's attention who is already interested in the topic your discussing (what your video is about). This will in all likelihood nudge the other users to view your profile/videos. Just as any other social network, the more connections you have, the more the word about your videos and business will get out there.

YouTube success story

As discussed earlier, the main benefit of getting your videos out on YouTube is that it give you the opportunity to "advertise" your business to millions of users, and at the rate of $0. Yes, Free 99. This gives the potential growth of your business an infinite amount. A great example of this is a blender company called Blendtec.

Blendtec became an internet sensation, mostly in thanks to YouTube. Blendtec is a company that sells heavy duty blenders. They created a simple, cheap video series (first video cost them $50 total) on YouTube displaying how well their blenders work. The names the series "Will It Blend?" They used their Blendtec blenders to blend random objects such as baseballs, golf balls, glow sticks, cell phones, magnets, etc. Now, this may sound like just a simple idea it was extremely effective. The following are the amount of views a couple of these videos have received: Glow sticks: 6.9 million views, iPhone: 9 million views, golf balls: 5.9 million views, magnets: 2.7 million views, baseball: 1.4 million views. Just these five examples produced 25.9 million views for this blender company. They have many more videos out there (producing over 100 million views), but I think you get the idea. According to CEO Tom Dickinson in his interview with inc.com, the company skyrocketed over 700% in value because of these videos.

As the above example demonstrates, the potential growth for your business due to YouTube video promotion is limitless. It is important to remember that YouTube allows you to promote video for FREE. Target the right audience, come up with interesting, creative videos and stick with it. Use all the tools YouTube provides for you to get that video out.

Promote/Embed/Link your video with all that you can. Getting your name out there is the name of the game.

Earn from your skills

How to freelance your proficiency

You can learn how to freelance since this is the best way you can improve your writing skills and at the same time earn money while you work from home. A freelancer works from home on contract basis, he or she is self employed and so the services they give earns them money. A freelancer can choose when to work, where to work and whom to work for.

Freelance writing is all about being an independent writer who does different projects which are from several companies, it also requires one to be committed and serious with the work they do. Aim high and have a target so as to be successful.

Some of the common fields in freelancing are: Website developer, Copy writing, Computer programming, Proof reading, Data entry, Graphic designer and many more.

Three reasons why you can freelance from home

- Time: you can freelance with ease and set your own working time. When you work from home as a freelancer you can work part time or full time. Freelancing also does not put any work strain on you because you choose the kind of assignment you think you can tackle.

- You can work from home: freelancing does not necessarily need an office. You can work at the comfort of your home. You only need basic technology that comes along with freelancing. Some of the things you require are a computer with internet connection, business email, word processing software, telephone, data security and the required skills depending on the tasks.

- You are your own boss: working from home as a freelancer, one needs to have top most discipline. You don't have a supervisor over you, so you have to remind yourself of the deadlines and even keep checking the progress of your work.

How to begin freelancing

If you have several skills, focus on at least two of your strongest points that you are skillful with and are frequently sought after services in the industry. Prepare a good resume; remember your portfolio tells much about your capabilities. If need be, you can hire a professional to prepare the resume at a fee. Including examples of work that you have done previously is an added advantage. Evaluating competition in the niche that you choose is vital because this will tell you the market size and the ability to take up new writers.

Where to find freelance assignments

The lists of freelance sites are coming out every day. Most of them are scams. For you to learn how to freelance and succeed, you need to find out the authenticity of the site before engaging one self. Most sites post their requirements of writers on their site. It is advisable to browse through various sites for topics of your skill.

Business models that will make you a well-paid freelance writer

A lot of money can be made as a freelance writer these days. The Internet, constantly expanding in size and functionality, becomes accessible to millions more people every year, opening up the door to a world of information. That information is communicated through words (for the most part) and those words have to come from somewhere - creating a huge opportunity for the modern-day writer.

And let me ask you something. How many people do you know who enjoy reading? Reading for pleasure, I mean. While many "snack" on information via websites and magazines, not many people spend time reading books anymore.

Why is that significant to you? Well, because talented writers usually develop their knack for writing, the "gift for language" most people assume they were born possessing, through a passion for reading.

So thanks to modern trends, the demand for written content is increasing even as the number of good writers out there decreases.

If you're one of the few who can write well and want to make some money out of your talent, here are some fields you may want to consider. Any one of them, with some hard work and business savvy, will make you a very comfortable individual.

So let's have a look

Blog Writing

Blog writing holds more potential than you will ever find in standard SEO articles because blog owners truly care about their projects. Blogs are meant to connect with an audience - not just push a website up in the search rankings, and the aim is to be a credible authority on the matter at hand.

Niche blogs make up a big part of the market. Subjects I've covered extensively for blogs include men's dating/seduction, world travel, personal development, green business, internet marketing, and physical fitness.

Industry professionals (contractors, real estate agents, psychologists, life coaches, etc) make up another large portion of the market-they use blogs to keep in touch with their prospective customers and establish credibility. Essentially, they use blogs for PR.

Blog owners with an eye for quality will pay anywhere from $25 to well over $100 per article, and most of the ones I work with order a minimum of 4 articles per week (though some clients are happy with many less). Even at the bottom rung of the pay scale I've mentioned, one average client amounts to $400 per month for about an hour of work every week.
Not too shabby.

Web Content Writing

Another form of high-paid writing is web content - not basic SEO content but the type of web content that builds a company's brand, describing their corporate culture, products, and services.
For higher-paying web content clients, seek out brick and mortar companies looking to use the internet to generate more leads.

These types of companies, accustomed to paying tens of thousands of dollars for advertising, demand high-quality work and will pay the price (unlike many online businesses). Non-profit organizations put a lot of credence into organizational image as well, possibly more so than businesses. Consider establishing a presence in your local community and networking, much like other local businesses do, to avoid competition from other online writers and get top rates.

Ebook/Report Writing

Writing eBooks and reports can generate loads of cash as well. Larger projects come with higher quality standards because your clients know the people they sell these books to expect their money's worth. Customers buy good eBooks and reports go for $15-$70 (often more; often less), so they expect value in their purchase; for this reason, a cheap SEO writer will not do.

Not to mention more time is needed to develop a concept for an eBook project and tie it all together in one tight package. Plenty of online marketers sell eBooks and reports for top dollar, and most don't like writing all that much. Premium writers step in and do that for them.

Article Syndication Writing

Stay away from basic article work because much of it is used for SEO and thus the pay tends towards the low-end. But you might want to consider clients who order articles for a completely different reason - article syndication.

These marketers realize the best way to build a business out of content is to write, or pay someone to write, for the readers. The objective of content written for syndication isn't to get backlinks but to get as many publishers as possible to publish it on their sites and in their ezines, building traffic to the marketer's site so they can make a sale.

Clients who use the article syndication model are willing to pay a lot more money because they know the kind of content that goes viral takes a lot of time to create.

Writing Offline Materials

Not all high-paid content writers work in the online world, and businesses were paying a premium for work published in print long before the Internet boomed. You don't have to famous to make money in print either. Once again, businesses (as well as non-profits) pay big money to build their company image, and herein lies your path to success.

Think brochures, menus, magazine advertisements, speeches, direct mail, and information packets (the list goes on and on). Check out the Writer's Market for the prices average writers charge for work of this nature.

Book Ghostwriting

Ghostwriters make a lot of money writing novels, memoirs, autobiographies, reports...you name it. A serious ghostwriting client will spend thousands upon thousands of dollars to get their book written. These projects take collaboration, time, and the most top-notch writing - indeed, ghostwriters must always be a perfect fit for their client.

Daunting, yes, but these are all reasons ghostwriting pays so well. As a warning, seeing someone else recognized for your work takes some real humility (a truth that somewhat applies to all markets). Also, be aware that, especially when browsing sites like Elance for work, dreamers who never really pull the trigger on their project make up the majority of potential prospects. Plenty of legitimate clients need work done too, but you need some real marketing savvy and knowledge of the industry to find and land them.

Copywriting

Sales copywriting is easily the most lucrative of all the writing fields; selling via written content is an art and science that takes a lot of practice to learn. Reputable copywriters get thousands of dollars for one single page of writing, but they put a lot of time into producing that one page.

Regardless, the money made relative to hours worked is fantastic. Top marketers are willing to pay big bucks for converting copy because they know the high level of skill needed is a rarity. The difference between a writer who understands the intricacies of effective copy and one who doesn't has a huge impact on the bottom line.

Never sell yourself as a sales writer unless you've had proper training or spend a lot of hours of self-study learning and practicing copywriting theory. John Carlton, the highest paid copywriter in the business, offers one of the best training programs out there. Just Google his name and you'll find his course.

Writing for Yourself

Finally, if you really want to make money as a writer, stop writing information products and marketing material for other people and go into business for yourself. Once you know how to create a good product, as well as put together the marketing content for driving eyeballs to an offer, why not reap all the rewards?

Sure, the money will not come in right away; it will take time. But if you get it right, the money will come, often in droves. And with the right business model, your creation will pay you again and again and again - true passive income.

You will, however, need a way to pay your living costs while getting started. Many writers get their foot in the door by offering their services first, saving up money while learning what business models work online from the people they work for, and then they build up online assets during their free time.
Not a bad plan at all...

Some examples the freelance sites include, ODesk and Elance

- ODesk - Do not be quick to bid for a low price on assignments. Take your time because new jobs are posted everyday. Exercise patience and you will see the benefits when the good paying jobs come along.

- Elance - This is so far the best site, the assignments are vast and the pay is high.

- Magazines - Though they do not pay much, they are quit good for a small beginning. You can start writing articles on magazines before your business grows to be an online freelancer.

Always remember to deliver good quality work on time, since there is a strong demand of quality freelancers.

How to freelance

The Assignment

Watch out on unworkable deadlines. If the deadlines are too soon be on the caution and also for jobs with remarks such as "It's really easy job". This could be a bait to get you into the scam.

The Compensation

As the saying goes, "when the deal is too good think twice". Generous payments are used to lure you into scams. Once you are in and the job is done you will never get paid. Some clients will promise to pay you after the delivery of the final product. It is good to withhold the delivery of the final product until payment is done.

The Client

Your qualification will determine the kind of assignment to do. If the client offers you a job of different qualifications it could be an indicator of a scam. A client that does not have contact should be avoided as quickly as possible.

8 ways to show you are a professional in freelancing

Learning how to freelance in a professional way is vital. Freelancer jobs are for professional candidates.

Before your potential clients give you an assignment, they try to figure out on which class you fall: the good or the bad class. The question here is, how can you show that you are a hard-working and a honest freelancer? Every little thing you do counts.

1. Have A Business Identity

Just like any other online home business, it is important to have a professional business identity.
A business identity consists of:
- Business Cards
- Well designed website
- A business logo

2. Your Pricing Should Be Set Up

Setting up your pricing structure early will help you when you are placing your freelance charges. This makes you not to overcharge or undercharge.

3. Present Your Previous Work

Be sure to present previous work from other clients if at all you have any. Incase you do not have any previous work; you can simply volunteer and obtain one, which can later boost your profile as a freelancer.

4. Show Your Clients Testimonials And Comments

Make sure your testimonials are real. It is important to include your previous clients detailed information, just in-case any one wants to find out the truth.

5. Confidence

Whenever you are talking to your clients, don't be unsure about yourself. Learn to be confident, because clients will buy your confidence before they buy your service.

6. Your Information Should Be Detailed In The Website

Most clients will want to know more about you before working with you as a freelancer. Adding your detailed information on your website will be an added advantage for you. This can give you a lot of credibility.

7. Dressing Code

Your dressing code is very important when dealing with your clients face to face. Your dressing code will tell much about you. Be neat in your overall appearance.

8. Be Willing To Say No

Turning down some requests that are not in your area of expertise make you look professional. You can not be a professional in every field. Choose exactly what you are experienced at.

5 factors to consider before charging your client in your freelance business

The biggest challenge in freelance business is how much you can charge your clients for your services.

The competition on freelancing is too high, so it is advisable not to overcharge because you will not get hired. On the other hand if you undercharge you will starve. Ideally, the best way is to be average while being competitive.

1. Level Of Skill And Experience

This goes without say, when you are well skilled in a particular area of business, you can charge more in your services, unlike when you are not well skilled. This is because the services rendered by both skilled and unskilled are really different.
On the other hand if you have more experience your charging rates are higher.

2. The Market Demand

When the demand is great your charges should be high. When there is too much work coming in it is always a sign of high demand. When you are really competing to get jobs is a sign of low demand which will make the charges go a little bit down.

3. Who Is Your Client

The Charges will always vary from client to client. Some clients are repeat customers, some jobs are riskier, and some really need a lot of effort and much more.

4. Your Take Home

Freelancing is business. Make sure you can be able to pay for your expenditures and atleast remain with a few dollars to take home. Regardless of the competition in the industry, you must ensure that the prices you choose are fair.

5. Size Of Your Business

A small business does not have much expense; it does not have great bills and also it does not have many employees to pay salary. This makes them feel comfortable charging a little bit lower. When the business is big, the charges will be higher because of the huge expenses that come along with it.

4 ways to keep your clients in your freelance business

1. Always Offer Excellent Service

The market is very competitive. Every client is looking out for the best services. No one wants to pay for anything that is average. Good services will boost your home business because you will get more clients.

2. Contact And Communication

Having the clients contact is important because it makes communication easy. You can talk to each other at any time should changes arise. When you communicate you keep them posted in your progress. Communication gives your clients peace of mind. Make sure you answer all the emails and phone calls from your clients. It is a way of building trust and letting them know that the deadline will be met by you.

3. Offer Incentives to Your Repeat Customers

Building a strong relationship with your regular clients is vital. You can offer them free incentives occasionally. By doing so, you make them feel appreciated and make them long for your services.

4. Ask About Client's Comments

Ask your clients on general view of your performance. Genuine clients will tell you if there is anything you should reflect on to make your business more favorable to their needs.
And by so doing you will build a good relationship with your clients and they can possibly come back for your services.

Mistakes to avoid as a freelancer

1. Saying "Yes" Always

Learn to say No when you find out that the client has a workload that you can not accomplish at their desired time.

2. Interruption

A freelancer has to be much disciplined in order to get their work done on time and accurately. Interruption like housework, internet surfing and television can hinder you from submitting quality work on time. Find a place that is quiet in order for you to concentrate.

3. Over Committing

Do not commit all your time to one client. You need time for your self; you need time to market your self, you need time to unwind and also time to catch up with your personal life.

4. Under pricing

You have the right to earn a fair price for your service. Learn to compare the volume of the assignment with the pay and see if it is worth. This is a major point to be considered especially if you have a family to look after.

5. Communication

Freelancing is one of the areas that are affected by scam. Sending and receiving emails is not a perfect substitute of one-to-one talk. Sometimes it is important to communicate with the clients' office so that you may know whom you are dealing with. Make sure that the company is legit before engaging your self. Find out what people are saying about the company.

6. Clarity

Time and time again freelancing contracts end up in disputes because of lack of clarity of terms in the very beginning. Get to understand and agree on the contract to avoid disputes with your client.

Freelance writing is about excellence and time keeping, this builds trust amongst the two parties.

Conclusion

The only person who can stop you from actualizing your dreams and maximizing your potentials is you. Never stop believing in your self and the things you can accomplish, trust me it's never too late to start and you're never a failure if you fail but you become one if and only if you stop trying. It's never too late to become that independent person you've always wanted to be.

BELIEVE IN YOURSELF, YOU CAN DO IT !!!